Adobe Flash/Animate CC Keyboard Shortcuts

By

U. C-Abel Books.

Table of Contents

Acknowledgement.

All thanks to God Almighty for enabling us to bring this work to this point. He is a wonder indeed.

We want to specially appreciate the great company, Adobe Systems for their hard work and style of reasoning in providing the public with helpful programs and resources, and for helping us with some of the tips and keyboard shortcuts included in this book.

Dedication

This book is proudly dedicated to every user of Adobe Flash/Animate.

How We Began.

We enjoy using shortcuts because they set us on a high plane that astonishes people around us when we work with them. As wonderful shortcuts users, the worst eyesore we witness in computer operation is to see somebody sluggishly struggling to execute a task through mouse usage when in actual sense shortcuts will help to save that person time. Most people have asked us to help them with a list of keyboard shortcuts that can make them work as smartly as we do and that drove us into research to broaden our knowledge and truly help them as they demanded, that is the reason for the existence of this book. It is a great tool for lovers of shortcuts, and those who want to join the group.

Most times the things we love don't come by easily. It is our love for keyboard shortcuts that made us to bear long sleepless nights like owls just to make sure we get the best out of it, and it is the best we got that we are sharing with you in this book. You cannot be the same at computing after reading this book. The time you entrusted to our care is an expensive possession and we promise not to mess it up.

Thank you.

What to Know Before You Begin.

General Notes.

1. Most of the keyboard shortcuts you will see in this book refer to the U.S. keyboard layout. Keys for other layouts might not correspond exactly to the keys on a U.S. keyboard. Keyboard shortcuts for laptop computers might also differ.

2. It is important to note that when using shortcuts to perform any command, you should make sure the target area is active, if not, you may get a wrong result. Example, if you want to highlight all texts you must make sure the text field is active and if an object, make sure the object area is active. The active area is always known by the location where the cursor of your computer blinks.

3. On a Mac keyboard, the Command key is denoted with the ⌘symbol.

4. If a function key doesn't work on your Mac as you expect it to, press the Fn key in addition to the function key. If you don't want to press the Fn key every time, you can change your Apple system preferences.

5. The plus (+) sign that comes in the middle of keyboard shortcuts simply means the keys are

meant to be combined or held down together not to be added as one of the shortcut keys. In a case where plus sign is needed; it will be duplicated (++).

6. Many keyboards assign special functions to function keys, by default. To use the function key for other purposes, you have to press Fn+the function key.

7. For keyboard shortcuts in which you press one key immediately followed by another key, the keys are separated by a comma (,).

8. For chapters that have more than one topic, search for "A fresh topic" to see the beginning of a topic, and "End of Topic" to see the end of a topic.

9. It is also important to note that the keyboard shortcuts, tips, and techniques listed in this book are for use in Adobe Flash/Animate CC.

10. To get more information on this title visit ucabelbooks.wordpress.com and search the site using keywords related to it.

11. Our chief website is under construction.

Some Short Forms You Will Find in This Book and Their Full Meaning.

Here are short forms used in this Adobe Flash/Animate CC Keyboard Shortcuts book and their full meaning.

1.	Win	-	Windows logo key
2.	Tab	-	Tabulate Key
3.	Shft	-	Shift Key
4.	Prt sc	-	Print Screen
5.	Num Lock	-	Number Lock Key
6.	F	-	Function Key
7.	Esc	-	Escape Key
8.	Ctrl	-	Control Key
9.	Caps Lock	-	Caps Lock Key
10.	Alt	-	Alternate Key

CHAPTER 1.

Fundamental Knowledge of Keyboard Shortcuts.

Without the existence of the keyboard, there wouldn't have been anything like keyboard shortcuts so in this chapter we will learn a little about the computer keyboard before moving to keyboard shortcuts.

1. Definition of Computer Keyboard.

This is an input device that is used to send data to computer memory.

Sketch of a Keyboard

1.1 Types of Keyboard.

  i. Standard (Basic) Keyboard.
  ii. Enhanced (Extended) Keyboard.

  i. **Standard Keyboard:** This is a keyboard designed during the 1800s for mechanical typewriters with just 10 function keys (F keys) placed at the left side of it.

  ii. **Enhanced Keyboard:** This is the current 101 to 102-key keyboard that is included in almost all the personal computers (PCs) of nowadays, which has 12 function keys, usually at the top side of it.

Function Keys

Numeric Keys

Alphabetic keys

1.2 Segments of the keyboard

- Numeric keys.
- Alphabetic keys.
- Punctuation keys.
- Windows Logo key.
- Function keys.
- Special keys.

Numeric Keys: Numeric keys are keys with numbers from **0 - 9**.

Alphabetic Keys: These are keys that have alphabets on them, ranging from **A** to **Z**.

Punctuation Keys: These are keys of the keyboard used for punctuation, examples include comma, full stop, colon, question marks, hyphen, etc.

Windows Logo Key: A key on Microsoft Computer keyboard with its logo displayed on it. Search for this on your keyboard.

Apple Key: This also known as Command key is a modifier key that you can find on an Apple keyboard. It usually has the image of an apple or command logo on it. Search for this on your Apple keyboard

Function Keys: These are keys that have **F** on them which are usually combined with other keys. They are F1 - F12, and are also in the class called *Special Keys*.

Special Keys: These are keys that perform special functions. They include: Tab, Ctrl, Caps lock, Insert, Prt sc, alt gr, Shift, Home, Num lock, Esc, and many others. Special keys differ according to the type of computer involved. In some keyboard layout, especially laptops, the keys that turn the speaker on/off, the one that increases/decreases volume, the key that turns the computer Wifi on/off are also special keys.

Other Special Keys Worthy of Note.

Enter Key: This is located at the right-hand corner of most keyboards. It is used to send messages to the computer to execute commands, in most cases it is used to mean "Ok" or "Go".

Escape Key (ESC): This is the first key on the upper left of most keyboards. It is used to cancel routines, close menus and select options such as **Save** according to circumstances.

Control Key (CTRL): It is located on the bottom row of the left and right hand side of the keyboard. They also work with the function keys to execute commands using Keyboard shortcuts (key combinations).

Alternate Key (ALT): It is located on the bottom row also of some keyboard, very close to the CTRL key on both side of the keyboard. It enables many editing functions to be accomplished by using some keystroke combinations on the keyboard.

Shift Key: This adds to the roles of function keys. In addition, it enables the use of alternative function of a particular button (key), especially, those with more than one function on a key. E.g. use of capital letters, symbols, and numbers.

1.3. Selecting/Highlighting With Keyboard.

This is a highlighting method or style where data is selected using the computer keyboard instead of a computer mouse.

To do this:

- Move your cursor to the text or object you want to highlight, make sure that area is active,
- Hold down the shift key with one finger,
- Then use another finger to move the arrow key that points to the direction you want to highlight.

1.4 The Operating Modes Of The Keyboard.

Just like the computer mouse, keyboard has two operating modes. The two modes are Text Entering Mode and Command Mode.

a. **Text Entering Mode:** this mode gives the operator/user the opportunity to type text.
b. **Command Mode:** this is used to command the operating system/software/application to execute commands in certain ways.

2. Ways To Improve In Your Typing Skill.

1. Put Your Eyes Off The Keyboard.

This is the aspect of keyboard usage that many don't find funny because they always ask. "How can I put my eyes off the keyboard when I am running away from the occurrence of errors on my file?" My aim is to be fast, is this not going to slow me down?

Of course, there will be errors and at the same time your speed will slow down but the motive behind the introduction to this method is to make you faster than you are. Looking at your keyboard while you type can make you get a sore neck, it is better you learn to touch type because the more you type with your eyes fixed on the screen instead of the keyboard, the faster you become.

An alternative to keeping your eyes off your keyboard is to use the "*Das Keyboard Ultimate*".

2. Errors Challenge You

It is better to fail than to not try at all. Not trying at all is an attribute of the weak and lazybones. When you make mistakes, try again because errors are opportunities for improvement.

3. Good Posture (Position Yourself Well).

Do not adopt an awkward position while typing. You should get everything on your desk organized or arranged before sitting to type. Your posture while typing contributes to your speed and productivity.

4. Practice

Here is the conclusion of everything said above. You have to practice your shortcuts constantly. The practice alone is a way of improvement. "Practice brings improvement". Practice always.

2.1 Software That Will Help You Improve Your Typing Skill.

There are several Software programs for typing that both kids and adults can use for their typing skill. Here is a list of software that can help you improve in your typing: Mavis Beacon, Typing Instructor, Mucky Typing Adventure, Rapid Tying Tutor, Letter Chase Tying Tutor, Alice Touch Typing Tutor and many more. Personally, I love Mavis Beacon.

To learn typing using MAVIS BEACON, install Mavis Beacon software to your computer, start with keyboard lesson, then move to games. Games like **Penguin Crossing, Creature Lab**, or **Space Junk** will help you become a professional in typing. Typing and keyboard shortcuts work hand-in-hand.

Sketch of a computer mouse

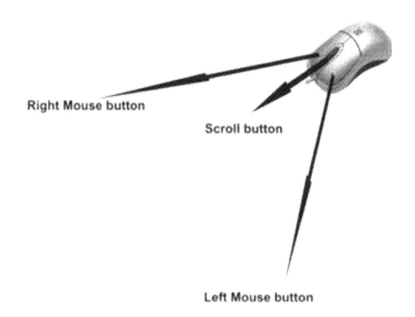

Right Mouse button

Scroll button

Left Mouse button

3. Mouse:

This is an oval-shaped portable input device with three buttons for scrolling, left clicking, and right clicking that enables work to be done effectively on a computer. The plural form of mouse is mice.

3.1 Types of Computer Mouse

- Mechanical Mouse.
- Optical Mechanical Mouse (Optomechanical).
- Laser Mouse.

- Optical Mouse.
- BlueTrack Mouse.

3.2 Forms of Clicking:

Left Clicking: This is the process of clicking the left side button of the mouse. It can also be called *clicking* without the addition of *left*.

Right Clicking: It is the process of clicking the right side button of a computer mouse.

Double Clicking: It is the process of clicking the left side button two times (twice) and immediately.

Triple Clicking: It is the process of clicking the left side button three times (thrice) and immediately.

Double clicking is used to select a word while triple clicking is used to select a sentence or paragraph.

Scroll Button: It is the little key attached to the mouse that looks like a tiny wheel. It takes you up and down a page when moved.

3.3 Mouse Pad: This is a small soft mat that is placed under the mouse to make it have a free movement.

3.4 Laptop Mouse Touchpad

This unlike the mouse we explained above is not external, rather it is inbuilt (comes with the laptop computer). With the presence of a laptop mouse touchpad, an external mouse is not needed to use a laptop, except in a case where it is malfunctioning or the operator prefers to use external one for some reasons.

The laptop mouse touchpad is usually positioned at the end of the keyboard section of a laptop computer. It is rectangular in shape with two buttons positioned below it. The two buttons/keys are used for left and right clicking just like the external mouse. Some laptops come with four mouse keys. Two placed above the mouse for left and right clicking and two other keys placed below it for the same function.

4. Definition Of Keyboard Shortcuts.

Keyboard shortcuts are defined as a series of keys, most times with combination that execute tasks which typically involve the use of mouse or other input devices.

5. Why You Should Use Shortcuts.

1. One may not be able to use a computer mouse easily because of disability or pain.

2. One may not be able to see the mouse pointer as a result of vision impairment, in such case what will the person do? The answer is SHORTCUT.

3. Research has made it known that Extensive mouse usage is related to Repetitive Syndrome Injury (RSI) greatly than the use of keyboard.

4. Keyboard shortcuts speed up computer users, making learning them a worthwhile effort.

5. When performing a job that requires precision, it is wise that you use the keyboard instead of mouse, for instance, if you are dealing with Text Editing, it is better you handle it using keyboard shortcuts than spending more time doing it with your computer mouse alone.

6. Studies calculate that using keyboard shortcuts allows working 10 times faster than working with the mouse. The time you spend looking for the mouse and then getting the cursor to the position you want is lost! Reducing your work duration by 10 times gives you greater results.

5.1 Ways To Become A Lover Of Shortcuts.

1. Always have the urge to learn new shortcut keys associated with the programs you use.
2. Be happy whenever you learn a new shortcut.

3. Try as much as you can to apply the new shortcuts you learnt.
4. Always bear it in mind that learning new shortcuts is worth it.
5. Always remember that the use of keyboard shortcuts keeps people healthy while performing computer activities.

5.2 How To Learn New Shortcut Keys

1. Do a research on them: quick references (a cheat sheet comprehensively compiled like ours) can go a long way to help you improve.
2. Buy applications that show you keyboard shortcuts every time you execute an action with mouse.
3. Disconnect your mouse if you must learn this fast.
4. Read user manuals and help topics (Whether offline or online).

5.3 Your Reward For Knowing Shortcut Keys.

1. You will get faster unimaginably.
2. Your level of efficiency will increase.
3. You will find it easy to use.
4. Opportunities are high that you will become an expert in what you do.
5. You won't have to go for **Office button**, click **New,** click **Blank and Recent**, and click **Create**

just to insert a fresh/blank page. **Ctrl +N** takes care of that in a second.

A Funny Note: Keyboarding and Mousing are in a marital union with Keyboarding being the head, so it will be unfair for anybody to put asunder between them.

5.4 Why We Emphasize On The Use of Shortcuts.

You may never leave your mouse completely unless you are ready to make your brain a box of keyboard shortcuts which will really be frustrating, just imagine yourself learning all shortcuts that go with the programs you use and their various versions. You shouldn't learn keyboard shortcuts that way.

Why we are emphasizing on the use of shortcuts is because mouse usage is becoming unusually common and unhealthy, too. So we just want to make sure both are combined so you can get fast, productive and healthy in your computer activities. All you need to know is just the most important ones associated with the programs you use.

CHAPTER 2.

15 (Fifteen) Special Keyboard Shortcuts.

The fifteen special keyboard shortcuts are fifteen (15) shortcuts every computer user should know.

The following is a list of keyboard shortcuts every computer user should know:

1. **Ctrl + A:** Control A, highlights or selects everything you have in the environment where you are working.

    *If you are like **"Wow, the content of this document is large and there is no time to select all of it, besides, it's going to mount pressure on my computer?"** Using the mouse for this is an outdated method of handling a task like selecting all, Ctrl+A will take care of that in a second.*

2. **Ctrl + C:** Control C copies any highlighted or selected element within the work environment.

   Saves the time and stress which would have been used to right click and click again just to copy. Use ctrl+c.

3. **Ctrl + N:** Control N opens a new window or file.

   Instead of clicking **File**, **New**, **blank/ template** *and another* **click**, *just press* **Ctrl + N** *and a fresh page or window will appear instantly.*

4. **Ctrl + O:** Control O opens a new program.

   Use ctrl +O when you want to locate / open a file or program.

5. **Ctrl + P:** Control P prints the active document.

   Always use this to locate the printer dialog box, and thereafter print.

6. **Ctrl + S:** Control S saves a new document or file and changes made by the user.

   Please stop! Don't use the mouse. Just press Ctrl+S and everything will be saved.

7. **Ctrl +V:** Control V pastes copied elements into the active area of the program in use.

Using ctrl+V in a case like this Saves the time and stress of right clicking and clicking again just to paste.

8. **Ctrl + W:** Control W is used to close the page you are working on when you want to leave the work environment.

> ***"There is a way Debby does this without using the mouse. Oh my God, why didn't I learn it then?"*** Don't worry, I have the answer. Debby presses Ctrl+W to close active windows.

9. **Ctrl + X:** Control X cuts elements (making the elements to disappear from their original place). The difference between cutting and deleting elements is that in Cutting, what was cut doesn't get lost permanently but prepares itself so that it can be pasted on another location defined by the user.

> *Use ctrl+x when you think **"this shouldn't be here and I can't stand the stress of retyping or redesigning it on the rightful place it belongs".***

10. **Ctrl + Y:** Control Y undoes already done actions.

> *Ctrl+Z brought back what you didn't need? Press Ctrl+ Y to remove it again.*

11. **Ctrl + Z:** Control Z redoes actions.

    Can't find what you typed now or a picture you inserted, it suddenly disappeared or you mistakenly removed it? Press Ctrl+Z to bring it back.

12. **Alt + F4:** Alternative F4 closes active windows or items.

    *You don't need to move the mouse in order to close an active window, just press **Alt + F4**. Also use it when you are done or you don't want somebody who is coming to see what you are doing.*

13. **Ctrl + F6:** Control F6 Navigates between open windows, making it possible for a user to see what is happening in windows that are active.

    Are you working in Microsoft Word and want to find out if the other active window where your browser is loading a page is still progressing? Use Ctrl + F6.

14. **F1:** This displays the help window.

    *Is your computer malfunctioning? Use **F1** to find help when you don't know what next to do.*

15. **F12:** This enables user to make changes to an already saved document.

    F12 is the shortcut to use when you want to change the format in which you saved your existing document, password it, change its name, change the file location or destination, or make other changes to it. It will save you time.

Note: The Control (Ctrl) key on Windows and Linux operating system is the same thing as Command (Cmmd) key on a Macintosh computer. So if you replace Control with Command key on a Mac computer for the special shortcuts listed above, you will get the same result.

CHAPTER 3.

Tips, Tricks, Techniques, and Keyboard Shortcuts for use in Flash/Animate.

About the program: This, formerly called Adobe Flash is an application developed by Adobe Systems that is used in developing rich contents, user interfaces, web contents such as video, audio, and multimedia, and rich internet application.

A fresh topic

Improving the Performance of your Adobe Flash or Animate.

By Dmitriy Yukhanov.

When developing applications with Adobe Flash Professional CS5 or later, it's important to consider strategies that can increase your application's performance and also improve the user experience. Over the past few years I've collected a series of best practices and pitfalls by working with developers on a variety of projects and also by researching the Flash documentation.

This topic offers some common Flash development rules that you may find useful in your own work. Feel free to follow these suggestions to create content more efficiently and optimize elements to ensure that your projects download quickly and run smoothly.

The tips described herein are useful not just for Flash developers but also for Flash animators and designers. Apply these approaches to your own projects to see how you can improve them.

Note: Throughout this topic, screen shots with a red border show what to avoid; green indicates what to follow.

Improving Performance.

This section includes helpful suggestions for making content play more seamlessly in Adobe Flash Player and use fewer resources.

Deactivate interactivity of unused objects with mouseChildren and mouseEnabled

If you're absolutely sure that objects in your Flash project will never be interactive (and will not contain any interactive objects), you can add the following code on the first frame of the object's containers:

mouseEnabled = false; mouseChildren = false;

This code deactivates the container and all nested containers inside it. To keep a container activated and interactive, use mouseChildren = false; only. Decreasing the number of active containers in a project helps increase performance because the movie uses fewer resources (see Figure 1).

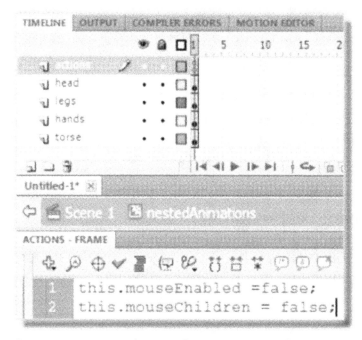

Figure 1. Use ActionScript to remove interactivity from objects on Stage.

Evaluate whether bitmaps or vectors are the best choice for each graphic asset

If the graphics in your project contain a lot of gradients, details, and colors, you may find after testing that bitmap images are the best choice to display the images on the Stage. When you use bitmap images, they are resolution-dependent and can look bad when scaled, but you may not need to scale the graphics. If they do require scaling, try using traced vector shapes to see if they can convey enough detail. Always make tests and compare the project's performance when using vector shapes and bitmap images to discover the best option in each case (see Figure 2).

Figure 2. Try using both vector and bitmap graphics to see what works best.

Convert outlines to fills using the Convert Lines to Fills option

Choose Modify > Shape > Convert Lines to Fills to convert shape outlines and vector lines to vector fills. Lines require more resources because they have two sides—compared to only one side in fills (see Figure 3).

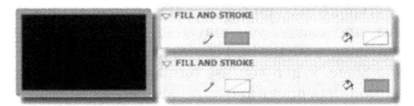

Figure 3. Use the Convert Lines to Fills option to improve performance.

Use non-solid line styles sparingly

Unless necessary, avoid adding dashed or dotted lines. Solid lines require fewer resources to draw (see Figure 4).

Figure 4. Use solid lines and strokes whenever possible.

Use lines instead of curves

When editing vector shapes, use miter joins instead of round joins. Miter joins are lines that require fewer resources compared to rendering curves. You should also use miter joins when displaying small vector shapes because rounded joins are not so noticeable and waste unneccessary resources (see Figure 5).

Figure 5. Use square miter joins for corners instead of rounded joins.

Optimize vector shapes

Complex <u>vector</u> shapes often contain many control points between lines and curves. By removing unneeded points, you can save resources without affecting a graphic's appearance. Choose Modify > Shape > Optimize (or use the Smooth tool) to optimize vector graphics. Strike a balance between vector complexity (shape quality) and reduced line count (see Figure 6).

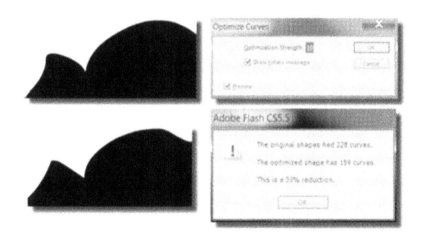

Figure 6. Reduce unnecessary points in vector artwork to save resources.

Avoid using vector gradient fills

Shapes filled with gradient fills require more resources compared to solid color fills. Whenever possible, replace gradient fills with solid fills. Although you only gain a small performance boost, this can be helpful when developing projects for mobile devices (see Figure 7).

Figure 7. Fill vector shapes with solid color fills.

Minimize the use of graphics with alpha transparencies

Alpha channel transparency really impacts performance, especially when applied to animated objects. Double-check PNG bitmap images to verify that they don't have unused alpha transparency settings when you imported them. Unless needed, don't set the alpha property on symbol instances as well—avoid creating fading animations in projects (see Figure 8).

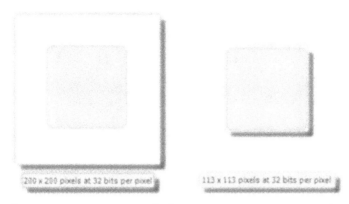

Figure 8. Remove alpha transparency settings unless they are necessary.

Only use masks when necessary

Identify situations when you must use masks, and try to use them sparingly. Whenever possible, crop images and vector graphics using an image-editing program, such as Adobe Illustrator or Adobe Fireworks, rather than cropping images with masks.

Masks require additional resources and hidden parts of the graphic increase file size unnecessarily. In some cases, you can replace rectangle masks with code functions. Programming with the scrollRect property uses fewer resources, but is not always suitable; it depends on the goal you are trying to achieve. Look for strategic ways to avoid using masks in your projects and explore new options that result in a similar appearance (see Figure 9).

Masked vector   Bitmap

Figure 9. Avoid masks if you can achieve similar effects with shapes or bitmaps.

Try to reduce use of blending modes on graphic elements

When you apply <u>blending</u>, it decreases a project's performance. Use an image editing program to prepare images and graphics to avoid using blending as much as possible (see Figure 10).

Figure 10. Prepare images with blend effects before importing them into Flash.

Minimize use of filters in Flash

Try to avoid using <u>filters</u> unless it is necessary to achieve a specific effect. Prepare images with shadows in an image editing program instead of applying shadow filter to images in Flash. Filters impact the project's performance in some cases (see Figure 11).

Figure 11. Add filter effects, like dropshadows, before importing images.

Use the lowest filter quality setting that results in an acceptable appearance

If your project doesn't require the higher settings, don't use the High and Medium quality. Test the Low Quality setting to see if it works well enough for your requirements. When you use the higher quality settings, you increase resources consumption (see Figure 12).

Figure 12. Use the Low Quality setting if it looks acceptable in your projects.

Resize bitmap images using even numbers if they are going to be downscaled

When scaling and cropping images in an image-editing program, to prepare them to be imported in Flash for downscaling, crop them to square dimensions using even number values.

You can also use <u>mipmapping</u> to calculate the optimal dimensions of the bitmaps you are creating. Mipmapping doesn't work on cached bitmap images (or bitmaps with filters applied). If you don't plan on downscaling a bitmap image, use an image-editing program to resize the bitmap graphic to the actual size needed prior to importing it into Flash.

Here are some sample dimensions:

- 1024 x 1024 pixels
- 512 x 512 pixels
- 256 x 256 pixels

Use lower frame rates

Test your project using different <u>frame rates</u> to find the lowest acceptable one. Many animations play smoothly at 24–30 fps. User interfaces for applications (that do not have animations) can often playback at 12 fps without noticeably affecting appearance. If your project plays intermittent animations and you want them to play smoothly, you can use ActionScript code to change the frame rate at runtime. When a project is set to use higher frame rates, Flash Player has less time to draw the elements on the Stage and process the code. Depending on the project, higher frame rates can result in decreased performance. Be sure to test the project to see what works best for your content (see Figure 13).

Figure 13. Adjust the frame rate in the Property inspector.

Avoid nesting movie clips

Use layers instead of movie clip containers to organize assets whenever possible. Decreasing the number of nested containers in a project increases its performance (see Figure 14).

Figure 14. Rather than nesting movie clips, organize assets in the layers of the Timeline.

Avoid animating objects with applied filters

When you apply <u>filters</u> to objects, they automatically adopt the cacheAsBitmap behavior. Animating filters, tweening filter properties, tweening transformations, and tweening color effects forces Flash Player to recache objects on every frame and reapply their filters—which leads to the extremely high consumption of resources (see Figure 15).

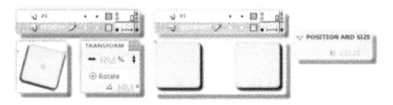

Figure 15. Animated filters, transformations, and color effects require more resources.

Note: You can animate the x and y properties of objects without recaching them.

Use powers of two when setting the Blur X and Blur Y filter properties

Calculate powers of two (2^1, 2^2, 2^3, etc.) when setting the Blur X and Blur Y filter properties in the Property inspector. Entering values like 2, 4, 8, or 16 can improve the speed that filters are applied by up to 20–30 percent (see Figure 16).

Figure 16. Enter powers of two when setting Blur X and Blur Y properties.

Cache complex vector graphics and text strategically

Use the Cache as Bitmap feature for complex vector graphics that do not contain nested animation. You can also apply it to static text fields. Use the Cache as Bitmap feature for objects that are not animated (or are animated only using the x and y properties)—including their parent containers.

If you are using ActionScript, you can also use cacheAsBitmapMatrix available in Adobe AIR only (starting with AIR 2). This enables you to scale and rotate cached objects without recaching so that the GPU (graphics card installed in the user's machine) composits and scales the transformations.

Additionally, you can use the Export as Bitmap feature introduced in Flash Professional CS5.5 to convert complex vector objects or nested objects into a bitmap graphic at the time the SWF file is compiled. Keep in mind that you have no control over the smoothing or compression settings applied to the exported bitmap images. Only use the Export as Bitmap feature on objects that do not contain nested animation. This mode has some added advantages over the classic Cache as Bitmap functionality. For example, exported images can be rotated, scaled, and animated as desired without incurring the same dramatic performance hit that occurs when working with cached objects. However, the exported bitmap images added to the SWF file do increase its file size.

If cached or exported bitmap objects have an opaque, continuous tone background fill, you should use the Opaque Bitmap background option and select a color to fill the background and gain even more performance improvements.

If a cached container includes a great deal of unused space between contained objects, make sure to cache each object individually to save extra bytes in memory. Try different strategies and compare the results to determine the best method to use (see Figure 17).

Figure 17. Choose the Display settings in the Property inspector.

Avoid using tween animations when creating very simple animations

You can use a programmatic approach to make simple animations such as movement, rotation, color changes, alpha transparency fading, and more. Explore using third-party libraries like TweenLite developed by GreenSock. This results in animations that save more resources and are more flexible to update (see Figure 18).

Figure 18. Replace tween animations with animations controlled by ActionScript.

Avoid using 2.5D in CPU mode

When you transform 3D objects using the user's computer's processor (CPU) instead of the graphics card (GPU), the project incurs the same performance issues as objects that use the Cached as Bitmap feature (see Figure 19).

Figure 19. Transformed 3D objects require greater processing resources.

Use redraw regions

You can use the option to show redraw regions in the context menu of the Debug Flash Player to see exactly which items are being drawn on the Stage (as well as when they appear). This strategy is helpful because you can find leftover invisible animations that are taking up unnecessary resources (see Figure 20).

Figure 20. Use the Show Redraw Regions option to see outlines of redrawn elements.

Strive to keep redraw areas as small as possible

Whenever possible, prevent regions from overlapping. The redraw regions of overlapping objects can merged into one larger region, which results in more empty space being redrawn. Smaller regions draw faster (see Figure 21).

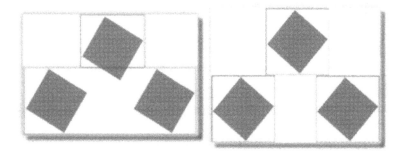

Figure 21. Overlapped elements can increase the size of redraw regions.

Always stop animations in hidden movie clips

If a movie clip contains animation that is played on demand (and not as the SWF loads) double-check that the animation is not running while the movie clip is hidden. Always stop animations when containers are hidden (or whenever you remove movie clips) to avoid using extra resources (see Figure 22).

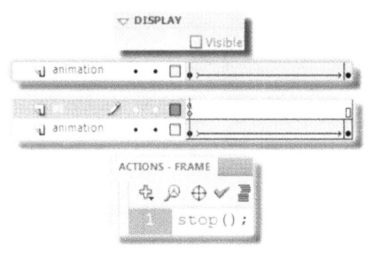

Figure 22. Add a stop action to ensure that hidden animations do not continue to play.

Avoid placing objects off the visible area of the Stage

Try not to place objects off the Stage area. If you change the Stage size and forget to remove them, the unseen graphics in the background will continue to consume resources while the SWF file plays. Also avoid keeping objects off the Stage in order to bring them onto the Stage later. It is better to use ActionScript code to set the visible property of the object to false and then set it to true—or add the object with the addChild() method—at the time you want the object to appear. Objects that are placed off the Stage, although not seen during playback, still consume resources (see Figure 23).

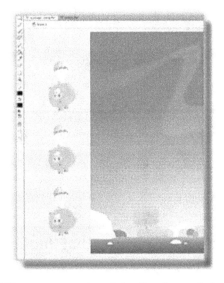

Figure 23. Avoid placing objects off the Stage area.

Avoid using TLF text fields unless you need specific text functionality

Use Classic text fields instead of TLF text fields unless your project specifically requires TLF text functionality. TLF text renders more slowly and adds more bytes to the SWF file compared to Classic text fields.

If you wish to add text features that are not included with Classic text fields, try using third-party TLF equivalents, such as TinyTLF. By default, imported text fields are set as TLF text fields. If you are not working with TLF text, remember to set them as Classic text fields in the Property inspector after importing them.

Choose the appropriate Preview Mode for each project

Change the document rendering quality to speed up its display. You can choose the most appropriate mode for your project by selecting View > Preview Mode (see Figure 24).

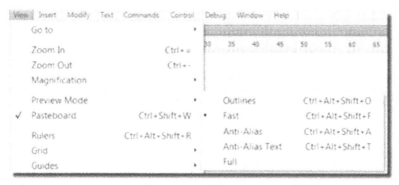

Figure 24. Experiment with using different preview modes for your projects.

Optimizing file size of project assets

Follow these suggestions to reduce the file size of the SWF files you create and improve their download times.

Set the appropriate compression on bitmap images

Carefully fine-tune the compression type and quality for every image in the Library using the Bitmap Properties dialog box, especially if you imported images created in Adobe Photoshop. This practice decreases the resources required and reduces the file size of the SWF file. If graphics contain many details, gradients, and colors, use JPEG compression; use PNG compression for less complex images to achieve a smaller SWF file size.

Avoid applying the Allow Smoothing option if possible because smoothing requires additional resources. Try to find a good balance between image quality and file size. Click the Test button to review the image's size and quality with the selected compression settings (see Figure 25); the quality is listed on the left side of the dialog box and the file size is listed at the bottom.

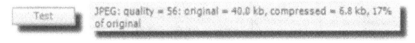

Figure 25. Click the Test button to see the quality and compression settings.

Consider when to fill shapes with bitmap images

You can break an image apart (Modify > Break Apart) or use the Color panel to set a shape's Color type to Bitmap fill. If you're only using part of the bitmap image to fill a shape, remember that the entire bitmap image will be compiled into SWF file when it is published.

Even though you're using only a few small pieces of the larger image, the entire image size will be added to the resulting SWF file. It's best to use an image editing program to prepare and import the smaller pieces as separate bitmap images and then use these smaller bitmap files as is, instead of to fill shapes.

Having said that, I think bitmap filling is a great strategy if you are using the entire bitmap image (or most of it) in multiple containers. In this case, you can use the bitmap fill feature to decrease the size of the SWF file because only one bitmap image will be compiled into the SWF file when it is published (see Figure 26).

Figure 26. Determine when it is most efficient to use bitmap fills for shapes.

Avoid scaling bitmap images

Whenever possible, use an image editing program to prepare images to avoid scaling them in Flash. Images that are scaled larger require additional resources. If you reduce the size of an imported image by scaling it down, you are adding unused bytes to the file size of the SWF file.

However, there are cases when you animate bitmap images in the Timeline to scale them smaller. In this situation, it is best to import the image at its largest size, prior to scaling (see Figure 27).

Figure 27. Resize images in an image editing program, and then import them.

Replace simple bitmap graphics with traced vector shapes

Use traced vector graphics in place of images with fewer colors, gradients, or details. When displaying simple graphics, <u>vector shapes</u> require fewer resources and result in a smaller SWF file size. If the source image is a bitmap image, you can convert the bitmap image to a vector shape with Illustrator. You can also choose Modify > Bitmap > Trace Bitmap in Flash. Always make tests compare performance when swapping out vector shapes for bitmap images to achieve the most efficient results (see Figure 28).

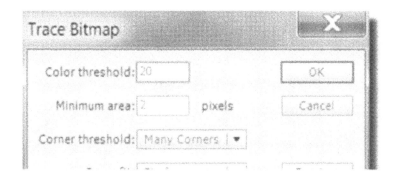

Figure 28. Use the Trace Bitmap feature in Flash to create vector shapes.

Replace frame-by-frame animations with tween animations

Whenever possible, use <u>tween</u> animations instead of frame-by-frame animations. In addition to saving time, the resulting SWF file may use fewer resources and result in a smaller SWF file size (see Figure 29).

Figure 29. Use tween animations rather than frame-by-frame animations.

Check the size report to identify assets in the project with larger file sizes

In the Publish Settings dialog box, enable the Generate Size Report option to learn if some of the elements in a Flash file are larger than expected. Identify larger files and attempt to optimize them or swap them out with smaller files.

Use symbols whenever possible

Whenever possible, convert graphic objects to symbols. Always convert graphic elements to symbols if the graphic asset is used more than once in the project. You can scale and apply color effects to symbol instances to create variations of the original graphic file. This strategy reduces the file size of the published SWF file.

Embed only the characters of a font you need to display in text fields

When working with dynamic, input, or TLF text fields, don't embed the entire character set of a font. Instead, embed only the characters that are used in the Flash project. This strategy avoids adding extra bytes to the SWF file. To embed fonts, choose Text > Font Embedding and be sure to name the embedded fonts with descriptive names to make the project easy to edit later (see Figure 30).

Figure 30. Use the Font Embedding dialog box to select only the characters needed to display the text in a project.

Disable the option to include XMP metadata in the Publish Settings dialog box

In the Publish Settings dialog box, disable the Include XMP Metadata option if the project does not use XMP metadata. This removes a few bytes from the published SWF file (see Figure 31).

Figure 31. Deselect the Include XMP Metadata option.

Developing Flash projects more elegantly

The suggestions described in this section improve the performance of your content. These practices facilitate changes, help you organize files, and make it easier to share your project files with other developers.

Avoid setting measurements to a twentieth of a pixel (twip)

Strive to set the x and y dimensions of every object rounded to whole integer values. This practice helps avoid various aliasing issues and also saves resources (see Figure 32).

Figure 32. Enter whole numbers for object property values.

Consider whether to use the Convert to Bitmap feature

The Convert to Bitmap feature (see Figure 33) enables you to convert vector elements and nested objects quickly into a single bitmap object. As it calculates the elements, it also takes into account any nested effects and masks. In some cases, it results in color loss or the addition of extra alpha during the conversion process.

Always check the resulting bitmap after completing the conversion. If you are finding that the results are not as expected, you can also consider taking a screenshot or using external image editing products to combine the elements, and then reimport the compiled bitmap file. Bitmap images created using the Convert to Bitmap feature are set to allow smoothing and Use PNG compression by default.

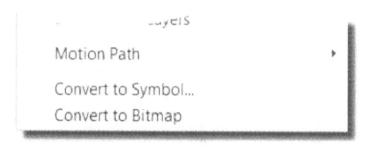

Figure 33. Always check images generated using the Convert to Bitmap option.

Use the Anti-alias for Animation font rendering option sparingly

Whenever possible, use the Anti-alias for Readability font rendering method unless you are animating a text field. The Anti-alias for Animation option results in fonts that are not as smooth as text using Anti-alias for Readability (see Figure 34).

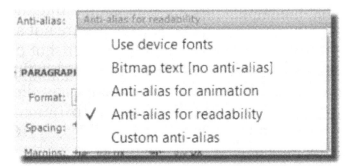

Figure 34. Set the Anti-alias for Readability option whenever possible.

Disable the Selectable option on text fields unless needed

The Selectable option on text fields is enabled by default. Disable this setting if it is not needed. It is a best practice to keep this setting enabled only if you think users will be copying the text in the text field, such as text fields that display error messages (see Figure 35).

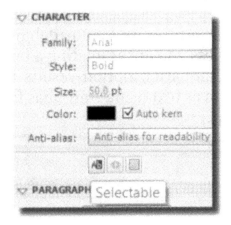

Figure 35. Remember to disable the Selectable option unless it is absolutely necessary.

Remove unused tween animations in the Timeline

Before publishing the final version of a project, review the Timeline to locate any tween animations that are not being used. Remove them using the "Remove tween" context menu and then publish the SWF file (see Figure 36).

Figure 36. Locate and delete any unused tween animations in the Timeline.

Hide objects strategically

Depending on the project goals, you can set the visible property of an instance to false as well as setting the object's alpha property to 0. For example, if you are programmatically causing an object to fade out, you can set its alpha value to 0. But once the animation is completed, be sure to also set the the object's visible property to false. Visible objects are still clickable and could block underlying items from receiving the user's mouse clicks. Additionally, visible objects, regardless of their alpha setting, consume more resources. If you simply want to hide an object without fading it out, set the visible property to false. In this case, it is not necessary to also change the object's alpha value.

To save more resources, completely remove objects from the DisplayList instead of hiding them. Programmatically show and hide them as needed, as long as the hide and show operations do not occur on every frame.

Avoid hiding objects under other objects on the Stage

If you wish to hide an object, set its visible property to false or remove it from the DisplayList. Objects hidden below other objects still wastes resources (see Figure 37).

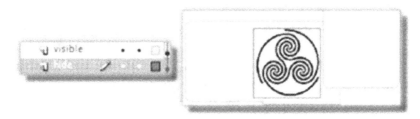

Figure 37. Set an object's visibility to false or remove it entirely; don't hide the object from view by placing it below other elements on the Stage.

Use custom UI components

Everything you can do to conserve resources and reduce file size improves the project— especially when developing for mobile devices. When you want to incorporate UI elements, such as a list menu, slider, or combo box, try using third-party components or develop underline custom UI elements yourself. Standard Flash components can consume too many resources to meet the requirements of some Flash applications (see Figure 38).

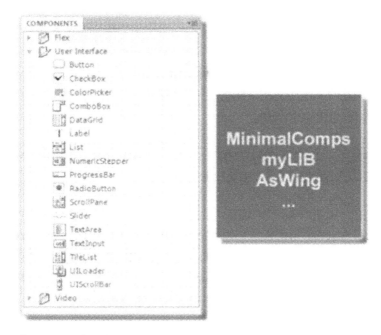

Figure 38. Create your own custom UI components built with ActionScript.

Name elements descriptively

Always enter meaningful, descriptive names to layers, fonts, and assets in the Library. This is a best practice because it helps you and other developers track bugs when debugging the project later (see Figure 39).

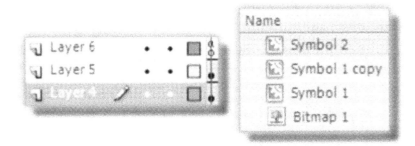

Figure 39. Don't use the default names assigned by Flash; enter names that describe each layer and element in the project.

Use only alpha-numeric characters, dashes, and underscores in names

Do not use spaces, capitalization, or special characters (even accented letters), especially from your native language (if it uses characters not used in the English alphabet). This is important because special characters in names can cause issues, including version control when using external tools.

Use consistent instance names for animated objects in the Timeline

If you've entered a name in the Instance Name field to reference an object in a tween animation on the Timeline, make sure to use the same instance name for all other instances of that object throughout the animation on the same layer. Doing so avoids several different issues that can occur if you are referencing the object with ActionScript code (see Figure 40).

Figure 40. Ensure that a named instance uses the same instance name throughout the entire layer.

Convert objects to movie clips before animating them

Always convert objects to symbols before animating them. If you don't work with symbols, the objects are automatically converted into graphic symbols (which cannot be named in the Property inspector, so they are useless when using ActionScript code). If you see items in the Library panel named "Tween1", "Tween2", and so on, this means that Flash converted objects that were not symbols into graphic symbols at the time they were tweened (see Figure 41).

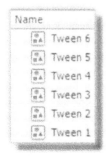

Figure 41. Always convert objects to symbols prior to animating them to avoid the automatic generation of graphic symbols.

Use the right text field type required for each situation

Consider the project requirements before choosing the type of text field to use. Choose the Static Text option if the text field does not have to be editable by the user or dynamically populated (or accessed) with ActionScript code. Use the Dynamic Text option if the text field's contents will be controlled using ActionScript. Choose the Input Text option if the text field must be editable by both the user and ActionScript code (see Figure 42).

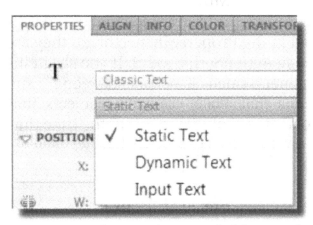

Figure 42. Choose the text field type that corresponds to your project requirements.

Choose the correct ActionScript type when creating and publishing files

If your project includes ActionScript 3 code, choose the ActionScript 3 option whenever you are creating new files or updating the Publish Settings. If you choose a different option (such as ActionScript 2) but the project contains ActionScript 3 code, it will not work and you may not immediately recognize why it appears to be broken (see Figure 43).

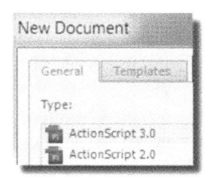

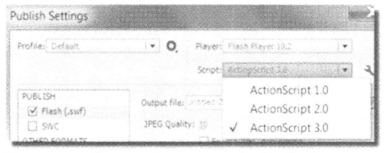

Figure 43. Choose the correct ActionScript type when creating and publishing files.

Use the publishing options that work best for each project

If a project uses an external library, consider using a SWC file instead of working with a set of AS files. Some

Flash developers choose to publish their projects as both SWC and a folder of AS files.

You can configure the Publish Cache settings (introduced in Flash Professional CS5.5) to specify your hardware. To access the Publish Cache settings, choose Edit > Preferences > Publish Cache.

If your project contains a lot of code and takes a long time to compile, you can disable the Warnings Mode option in the Publish Settings. Select the Flash tab, and then click the Advanced ActionScript 3.0 Settings while ActionScript 3 is selected, and then deselect the Warnings Mode check box. This option can result in a faster publishing process. However, keep in mind that when you disable the warning messages, you won't see code tips that are helpful when debugging projects (see Figure 44).

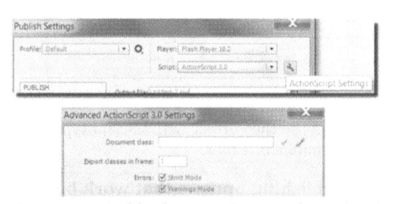

Figure 44. Disable the Warnings Mode option in the Publish Settings dialog box.

Making project files easier to update

Consider applying these best practices as you develop applications in Flash Professional. You can organize projects and set up elements to ensure that you and other team members can quickly update them later.

Place ActionScript and frame labels on the first two layers in the Timeline

Don't write your code on layers that contain project assets. If you do, you are hiding it from other developers (and yourself) when the Flash file is edited later. Place all code on its own, separate layer and place all frame labels on their own layer. Both layers should be located at the top of the layers stack in the Timeline, and locked to avoid accidentally adding assets to the layers that contain ActionScript code or frame labels (see Figure 45).

Figure 45. Isolate ActionScript code and frame labels on the first two layers.

Use frame labels rather than hard-coding frame numbers in scripts

Use labels with meaningful names instead of referring to frame numbers. This strategy helps avoid issues that can occur if an animation's length changes. It also makes it much easier to edit the Flash project later, and to help other developers understand how the project is set up (see Figure 46).

Figure 46. Use frame labels that describe the project, rather than referencing the frame by its number in the Timeline.

Avoid using bitmap images for text elements

It is much more difficult to edit text in bitmap files compared to editing text in text fields. When you import text, don't choose the Flattened Bitmap Image option; select the Editable Text option instead (see Figure 47).

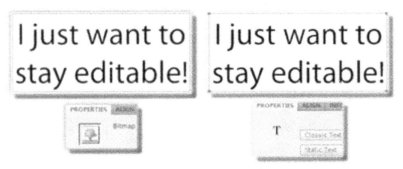

Figure 47. Use text fields, rather than bitmap images, for text elements.

Remove unnecessary keyframes from the Timeline

Keep track of unused keyframes and remove them from the Timeline. If you previously inserted keyframes, but they are no longer used to make any changes, you should remove them. In addition to wasting resources, empty keyframes can add confusion later when editing the project (see Figure 48).

Figure 48. Delete unnecessary keyframes in layers.

Make all layers in the Timeline the same length

Press F5 to insert additional frames to shorter layers and make them the same length as the longest layer. This is a best practice and keeps the Timeline easier to read (see Figure 49).

Figure 49. Extend all layers to match the length of the longest layer in the Timeline.

Delete empty, unused layers

Delete layers that do not contain any assets, ActionScript code, frame labels, audio elements, or other project elements. Empty layers can cause confusion and make editing the Timeline unnecessarily difficult (see Figure 50).

Figure 50. If layers are not needed, delete them from the Timeline.

Avoid using multiple scenes

Rather than working with scenes created in the Scenes panel, consider using movie clips or jumping to frames in the main Timeline instead. When you use multiple scenes, it can make the Flash file confusing to edit, particularly if you are sharing project files with other developers. Additionally, multiple scenes often cause increased size in published SWF files (see Figure 51).

Figure 51. Use frame labels and ActionScript to jump to sections in the main Timeline.

Name and use groups consistently, and only when needed

Groups make it easy to work with multiple objects simultaneously. Grouping is helpful when achieving tasks, such as aligning a group of objects to the Stage. You can group objects without impacting the performance of projects because groups are ignored when the SWF file is published.

However, if you are working on a project with a team of developers, it is a best practice to avoid grouping objects unnecessarily. It is much more elegant to use movie clips as containers for a set of related objects, because the team members can access the elements in a movie clip more easily. Objects that are grouped together may be more difficult to edit (see Figure 52).

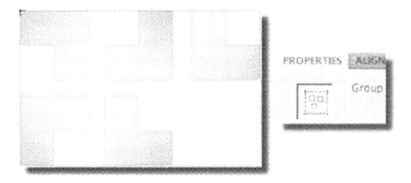

Figure 52. If you need to group objects to align them, ungroup them again after aligning the objects on the Stage.

Periodically check the Timeline to ensure tween animations remain unbroken

If a tween animation looks different in the Timeline (the solid line is now displaying a dashed line between frames), it means that the tween is broken. Usually this occurs because the objects used to create the animation are no longer on the Stage and are missing from one of the keyframes. In this case, delete the animation and recreate it (see Figure 53).

Figure 53. If you see dashed lines in the tween spans, it means the tween animation is broken.

Remove unused items from the Library panel

Make a backup copy of the FLA file and then remove all unused items (elements that are not used now and won't be used in future) to organize the Library panel and make the list of assets easier to read. This practice also ensures that the FLA project file is smaller.

In the Library panel, the Use Count feature is helpful for identifying unused elements. You can also choose Select Unused Items, but be careful when selecting this menu item because occasionally it includes files that are used in the project (see Figure 54).

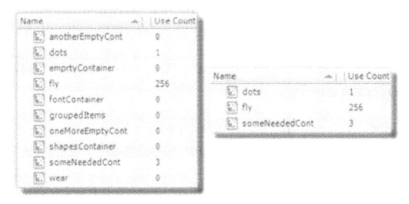

Figure 54. Review the Use Count column to identify elements that are not used in the project.

Create folders in the Library to organize related asset files

You can use folders to manage the contents of the Library panel and keep it well structured. Projects that use folders to organize assets are easier and faster to update (see Figure 55).

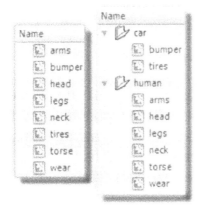

Figure 55. Create folders in the Library panel to organize project assets.

Update text field properties to match the project's design

By default, text fields are set to use a line spacing of 2 and multiline behavior. If your project only requires a single line text field with a line spacing of 0, update the options in the Property inspector to match the text field settings for your project (see Figure 56).

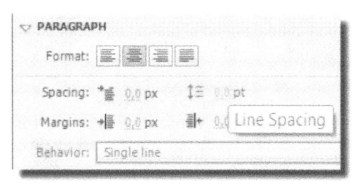

Figure 56. Use the Property inspector settings to update the selected text field

Don't break text fields apart

After you break apart text fields, they are no longer editable. If you are using the break apart feature to animate characters in a text field, consider using ActionScript to achieve the same effect. If you programmatically animate the text characters, the text field remains editable and is much easier to change when needed (see Figure 57).

Figure 57. Avoid breaking apart text fields because they cannot be edited.

Maintain the editability of text fields during the import process

When you import text fields, always choose the option to import them as Editable text (see Figure 58).

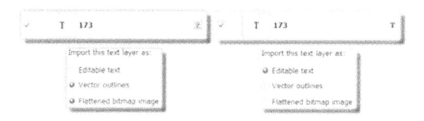

Figure 58. Choose the Editable text option in the Import dialog box.

Resize text field elements to match the size of their contents

Avoid leaving static text fields larger than the text contents inside them. Unless you have a specific reason—such as using text fields to display button labels—it's a best practice to use centered text alignment. It is much easier to edit text content later if the text is center-aligned and the text field's dimensions fit the text content inside.

To set the text field's dimensions to match the text content, click the white square icon in the top-right corner of the text field while editing the text. If a circle icon is displayed instead of a square icon, it means that the dimensions of the text field already match the text content that it contains (see Figure 59).

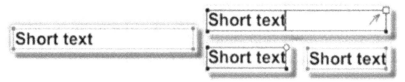

Figure 59. Resize the text field to match the text content and set the alignment of the text to align center.

Never attach ActionScript 2 code to buttons and movie clips

If you're working with a project that uses ActionScript 2 code, avoid attaching the code to objects. Always add the code as frame scripts because it is much easier to locate later (see Figure 60). You can identify frames that contain code because they display a lowercase character in the Timeline.

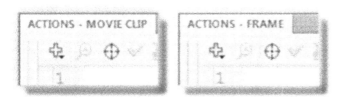

Figure 60. Add ActionScript 2 code to frame scripts.

Note: When you develop using ActionScript 3, you can only add the code to frames.

Organize project assets to keep font files easy to access

Always store font files in the project folder. When you need to share project files, be sure to include all the necessary files, including the font files used in the project.

Include all project libraries and third-party classes when you share a project

Don't forget to attach all external libraries and class files that are used in the project. Double-check that you are using global paths to link to external files.

Add ActionScript code to one centralized location in the project file

When adding ActionScript code to frames, try to organize all of the important scripts (needed for Stage resize handling, Stage setup, and more) in a location that is easy to access. This strategy makes it much easier to update the project file later. Generally speaking, it is a best practice to place important code on Frame 1 of the Actions layer so that any developer who works with the project in the future can quickly find it.

You can add the less important, isolated, or supplemental code in other locations that are controlled by this main script on Frame 1.

Use relative paths to external files

Use relative paths to classes, libraries, and output files. This makes your project portable and simple to share with other developers. If you always follow this rule, other team members won't have to change the paths later (see Figure 61).

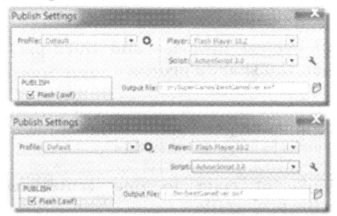

Figure 61. Use relative paths when linking to external files.

Where to go from here

I hope that the tips provided in this topic will help you create optimized Flash projects. By applying these suggestions to your development workflow, you can improve the performance of Flash animations and provide better user experiences on both desktop and mobile devices.

Additionally, by incorporating these best practices, you can ensure that your files are easier to update and manage in the future. This is especially helpful when working within a team.

If you have other Flash tips to share, especially if they solve a specific problem, please add them to the Flash cookbook.

This was by Dmitriy Yukhanov.

End of Topic.

A fresh topic

Keyboard Shortcuts in Flash/Animate.

You can create and modify keyboard shortcuts in Animate.

Customize keyboard shortcuts

1. Select (Windows) Edit > Keyboard Shortcuts or (Macintosh) Animate > Keyboard Shortcuts.

   The Keyboard Shortcuts dialog box appears.

2. Use the following options to add, delete, or edit keyboard shortcuts:

   Keyboard Layout Presets

   Lets you choose a preset of predetermined shortcuts from the drop-down, or any custom set you may have defined.

   Search

   Lets you search for any command whose shortcut you want to set or modify. Alternatively, you may drill-down the command within the tree view of commands.

   Match Case

   Lets you perform a case-sensitive search of the command.

   Add

   Adds a new shortcut to the selected command. To add a new keyboard shortcut for the selected command, click Add and enter a new key combination. Each command can one keyboard shortcut each; if a shortcut is already assigned to a command, the Add button is disabled.

Undo

Undo the last set shortcut for a command.

Copy to clipboard

Copy the entire list of keyboard shortcuts to clipboard of your Operating System.

Go To Conflict

Navigates to conflicting command. In case of a conflict when setting up a shortcut, a warning message is displayed.

Save shortcuts to a preset

Save the entire set of shortcuts to a preset. Presets can then be selected from the Keyboard Layout Presets drop-down.

Delete Shortcut

Deletes a selected shortcut.

Note:

You cannot use single keys such as delete or page up, ones that are pre-defined for some generic tasks such as deleting content, page scrolling, etc.

3. Click OK.

Remove a shortcut from a command

1. From the Commands pop-up menu, select a command category, select a command from the Commands list.
2. Click the X mark beside the shortcut.

Add a shortcut to a command

1. From the Commands pop-up menu, select a command category and select a command.
2. Click the Add button.
3. Press a key combination.

Note:

If a conflict occurs with the key combination (for example, if the key combination is already assigned to another command), an explanatory message appears just below the Commands list. Click the Go To Conflict button to quickly navigate to the conflicting command, and change the shortcut.

4. Click Ok.

Edit an existing shortcut

1. From the Commands pop-up menu, select a command category, select a command from the Commands list.
2. Double-click the shortcut.
3. Press a new key combination.

Note:

If a conflict occurs with the key combination (for example, if the key combination is already assigned to another command), an explanatory message appears just below the Commands list. Click the Go To Conflict button to quickly navigate to the conflicting command, and change the shortcut.

Use the following list of keyboard shortcuts to enhance your productivity in Adobe Animate.

Result	Mac Shortcut	Windows Shortcut
Import Image/Sound/etc...	Command + R	Ctrl + R

Export to .swf/.spl/.gif/, and so on	Command + Shift + R	Ctrl + Shift + R
Open as Library	Command + Shift + O	Ctrl + Shift + O

View.

Result	Mac Shortcut	Windows Shortcut
View movie at 100% size	Command + 1	Ctrl + 1
Show Frame	Command + 2	Ctrl + 2
Show All	Command + 3	Ctrl + 3

Windows.

Result	Mac Shortcut	Windows Shortcut
Show/Hide Library	Command + L	Ctrl + L
Modify Movie Properties	Command + M	Ctrl + M
Toggle between Edit Movie and Edit Symbol Mode	Command + E	Ctrl + E
Show/Hide Work Area	Command + Shift + L	Ctrl + Shift + L

Show/Hide Timeline	Command + Shift + W	Ctrl + Shift + W

Edit and Modify.

Result	Mac Shortcut	Windows Shortcut
Group	Command + G	Ctrl + G
Ungroup	Command + U	Ctrl + U
Break Apart	Command + B	Ctrl + B
Paste in Place	Command + Shift + V	Ctrl + Shift + V
Duplicate	Command + D	Ctrl + D
Select All	Command + A	Ctrl + A
Deselect All	Command + Shift + A	Ctrl + Shift + A
Optimize Curves	Command + Shift + O	Ctrl + Shift + O
Align Window	Command + D	Ctrl + D
Scale and Rotate	Command + Shift + S	Ctrl + Shift + S
Remove Transform	Command + Shift + Z	Ctrl + Shift + Z
Move Ahead	Command + Arrrow up	Ctrl + Arrrow up
Move Behind	Command + Arrrow down	Ctrl + Arrrow down

Bring to Front	Command + Shift+ Arrrow up	Ctrl + Shift + Arrrow up
Send to Back	Command + Arrrow down	Ctrl + Shift + Arrrow down
Modify Font	Command + T	Ctrl + T
Modify Paragraph	Command + Shift + T	Ctrl + Shift + T
Narrower letter spacing (kerning)	Command + Arrrow left	Ctrl + Arrrow left
Wider letterspacing (kerning)	Command + Arrrow right	Ctrl + Arrrow right

Miscellaneous Actions.

Result	Mac Shortcut	Windows Shortcut
Remove rotation or scaling from the selected objects	Command + Shift + Z	Ctrl + Shift + Z
Rotate the selection to 90 degrees left	Command + Shift + 7	Ctrl + Shift + 7

Scale and/or rotate the selection using numeric values	Command + Shift + S	Ctrl + Shift + S
Auto formats the editor code	Command + Shift + F	Ctrl + Shift + F
Show hidden characters	Command + Shift + 8	Ctrl + Shift + 8
suppresses highlighting of selected items	Command + Shift + E	Ctrl + Shift + E
Show or hide the pasteboard that surrounds the stage	Command + Shift + W	Ctrl + Shift + W
Show or hide the rulers	Command + Shift + Alt + R	Ctrl + Shift + Alt + R
Show Frame Script Navigator	Command + Alt + [	Ctrl + Alt + [

Show or hide the tweening shape hints	Command + Alt + I	Ctrl + Alt + I
Show a smaller area of the drawing with more detail	Command + =	Ctrl + =
Show a larger area of the drawing with less detail	Command + -	Ctrl + -
Show or hide the Align panel	Command + K	Ctrl + K
Show or hide the Color panel	Command + Shift + 5	Ctrl + Shift + 5
Show or hide the Compiler Errors panel	Command +Alt + 8	Ctrl +Alt + 8
Add Component Widgets	Command + 3	Ctrl + 3

Open a new window in the front most simulation that is a duplicate of the active window	Command + Alt + K	Ctrl + Alt + K
Show or hide the History panel	Command + T	Ctrl + T
Show or change the properties and position of the selected object	Command + I	Ctrl + I
Show or hide the Library panel for this document	Command + L	Ctrl + L
Show or hide the Property Inspector	Command + 9	Ctrl + 9

Show or change a list of the scenes in the current movie	Command + Shift	Ctrl + Shift
Select colors from swatches and manage swatches	Command + 5	Ctrl + 5
Show or hide the animation timeline and layers controls	Command + Alt + T	Ctrl + Alt + T
Show or hide the drawing toolbar	Command + 8	Ctrl + 8
Scale and/or rotate the selection using numeric values	Command + T	Command + T
Shifts the entire range of onion	Command + drag towards left	Shift + drag towards left

skin markers to the left		
Shifts the entire range of onion skin markers to the right	Command + drag towards right	Shift + drag towards right

Applies to: *Adobe Flash/Animate CC.*

Customer's Page.

This page is for customers who enjoyed Adobe Flash/Animate CC Keyboard Shortcuts.

Our beloved and respectable reader, we thank you very much for your patronage. Please we will appreciate it more if you rate and review this book; that is if it was helpful to you. Thank you.

Download Our EBooks Today For Free.

In order to appreciate our customers, we have made some of our titles available at 0.00. They are totally free. Feel free to get a copy of the free titles.

Here are books we give to our customers free of charge:

(A) For Keyboard Shortcuts in Windows check:

Windows 7 Keyboard Shortcuts.

(B) For Keyboard Shortcuts in Office 2016 for Windows check:

Word 2016 Keyboard Shortcuts For Windows.

(C) For Keyboard Shortcuts in Office 2016 for Mac check:

OneNote 2016 Keyboard Shortcuts For Macintosh.

Follow this link to download any of the titles listed above for free.

Note: Feel free to download them from our website or your favorite bookstore today. Thank you.

Other Books By This Publisher.

Titles for single programs under Shortcut Matters Series are not part of this list.

S/N	Title	Series
Series A: Limits Breaking Quotes.		
1	Discover Your Key Christian Quotes	Limits Breaking Quotes
Series B: Shortcut Matters.		
1	Windows 7 Shortcuts	Shortcut Matters
2	Windows 7 Shortcuts & Tips	Shortcut Matters
3	Windows 8.1 Shortcuts	Shortcut Matters
4	Windows 10 Shortcut Keys	Shortcut Matters
5	Microsoft Office 2007 Keyboard Shortcuts For Windows.	Shortcut Matters
6	Microsoft Office 2010 Shortcuts For Windows.	Shortcut Matters
7	Microsoft Office 2013 Shortcuts For Windows.	Shortcut Matters
8	Microsoft Office 2016 Shortcuts For Windows.	Shortcut Matters
9	Microsoft Office 2016 Keyboard Shortcuts For Macintosh.	Shortcut Matters
10	Top 11 Adobe Programs Keyboard Shortcuts	Shortcut Matters
11	Top 10 Email Service Providers Keyboard Shortcuts	Shortcut Matters
12	Hot Corel Programs Keyboard Shortcuts	Shortcut Matters

13	Top 10 Browsers Keyboard Shortcuts	Shortcut Matters
14	Microsoft Browsers Keyboard Shortcuts.	Shortcut Matters
15	Popular Email Service Providers Keyboard Shortcuts	Shortcut Matters
16	Professional Video Editing with Keyboard Shortcuts.	Shortcut Matters
17	Popular Web Browsers Keyboard Shortcuts.	Shortcut Matters

Series C: Teach Yourself.

1	Teach Yourself Computer Fundamentals	Teach Yourself
2	Teach Yourself Computer Fundamentals Workbook	Teach Yourself

Series D: For Painless Publishing

1	Self-Publish it with CreateSpace.	For Painless Publishing
2	Where is my money? Now solved for Kindle and CreateSpace	For Painless Publishing
3	Describe it on Amazon	For Painless Publishing